Wireless Smart Home Control System with Future Update Capability

Safa Hamdare

Wireless Smart Home Control System with Future Update Capability

Technology to Keep You Connected to Your Home from Anywhere across the Globe

LAP LAMBERT Academic Publishing

Impressum / Imprint

Bibliografische Information der Deutschen Nationalbibliothek: Die Deutsche Nationalbibliothek verzeichnet diese Publikation in der Deutschen Nationalbibliografie; detaillierte bibliografische Daten sind im Internet über http://dnb.d-nb.de abrufbar.

Alle in diesem Buch genannten Marken und Produktnamen unterliegen warenzeichen-, marken- oder patentrechtlichem Schutz bzw. sind Warenzeichen oder eingetragene Warenzeichen der jeweiligen Inhaber. Die Wiedergabe von Marken, Produktnamen, Gebrauchsnamen, Handelsnamen, Warenbezeichnungen u.s.w. in diesem Werk berechtigt auch ohne besondere Kennzeichnung nicht zu der Annahme, dass solche Namen im Sinne der Warenzeichen- und Markenschutzgesetzgebung als frei zu betrachten wären und daher von jedermann benutzt werden dürften.

Bibliographic information published by the Deutsche Nationalbibliothek: The Deutsche Nationalbibliothek lists this publication in the Deutsche Nationalbibliografie; detailed bibliographic data are available in the Internet at http://dnb.d-nb.de.

Any brand names and product names mentioned in this book are subject to trademark, brand or patent protection and are trademarks or registered trademarks of their respective holders. The use of brand names, product names, common names, trade names, product descriptions etc. even without a particular marking in this work is in no way to be construed to mean that such names may be regarded as unrestricted in respect of trademark and brand protection legislation and could thus be used by anyone.

Coverbild / Cover image: www.ingimage.com

Verlag / Publisher:
LAP LAMBERT Academic Publishing
ist ein Imprint der / is a trademark of
OmniScriptum GmbH & Co. KG
Heinrich-Böcking-Str. 6-8, 66121 Saarbrücken, Deutschland / Germany
Email: info@lap-publishing.com

Herstellung: siehe letzte Seite /
Printed at: see last page
ISBN: 978-3-659-64988-2

Zugl. / Approved by: Mumbai, University of Mumbai, 2011

TABLE OF CONTENTS

LIST OF FIGURES:

LIST OF TABLES:

CHAPTER 1

INTRODUCTION

1.1 Problem Definition

The objective of this project is to provide tools and services that empower and enable people themselves to address their social, rational, and emotional needs. Equality, autonomy, and control are the goals of empowering design. Current smart home devices can be accessed by its remote control, within a limited coverage span of a personal area network, normally at around a 100m radius [4]. This project suggests solution for limited coverage problem. Instead this design is utilizing Internet, so the access coverage of a smart home device will be rendered virtually limitless, increasing convenience and operating devices of potential advancements in smart home technologies. Also enabling users to use data and functions stored in/served by their home PC from anywhere with GPRS enabled mobile devices. This is an added benefit of the design because users can access the data/functions at any time they want without carrying heavy notebook PC.

The system for controlling home appliances remotely have used web server as the interface between user and home network. There are two modules of this system wherein the home device is connected to the serial port of the computer through the interfacing switching circuit. First module requires a fix IP (Internet Protocol) address and remote user require high-speed connection in order to access the web interface and other interactive components of the web. Second module, where GUI (graphical user interface) is hosted on web server and can be accessed on a GPRS enabled mobile phone through a mobile application. The implementation to test the system has been done using Net Beans.

1.2 Relevance of the Project

Smart homes obviously have the ability to make life easier and more convenient. Who wouldn't love being able to control lighting, entertainment and

1

temperature from their couch? Home networking can also provide peace of mind. Whether you're at work or on vacation, the smart home will alert you to what's going on, and security systems can be built to provide an immense amount of help in an emergency. For example, not only would a resident be woken with notification of a fire alarm, the smart home would also unlock doors, dial the fire department and light the path to safety.

The effectiveness of smart home technology in home care situations depends on the acceptance and use of the technology by both users and end-users [10]. The intention to use the proposed system is therefore based on the extent to which people believe that the system will help them perform their job better. The goal of technology implementation in home quality service is to increase the well-being of residents, their autonomy and independence, increase their sense of security, and to relieve the (informal) care. If the technology supports these goals, then people perceive the technology as useful.

1.3 Scope of the Project

The key drivers for this application will be ease of use and the penetration of network enabled home device/appliance. The primary business opportunity will be to bundle home automation services with other residential services. While the ability to automate the home is unlikely to be compelling to most consumers from a stand-alone perspective, it could be very interesting when combined with services that have a clear consumer utility.There is lots of interest from the industry on the Smart Home market in the last decade.

Many people agreed the market did not really take off in the past as not many home owners are willing to pay a premium on smart home systems. There are other obstacles such as Low consumer awareness, fear of technologies, and lack of industry standards. The smart home market is concentrated on the small niche high-end market and the penetration of smart home system in the overall residential market is still on very low.

The goal of equipping the home environment with technology isn't just to automate all the tasks that are carried out by the residents. The objective in design is to provide tools and services that empower and enable people themselves to address their social, rational, and emotional needs. Furthermore technology is not the solution to create a perfect home environment but has the ability to make a useful contribution. The environment as a whole, including for instance social contacts and location of the home, is responsible for the overall satisfaction of the residents. Once logged-in the software enables the user to view current state of the device, if needed the user can update the device status at the same time or at a specified time in the future, right in a standard web browser. The performance of the software is satisfactory.

Few constraints of the project are:

1. Password protection is used to block the unauthorized.
2. Additional appliances can be added to the network through administrator, with no major changes to its core.
3. Internet Connection is required.
4. GPRS enabled mobile Phone is needed.
5. Java Run time Environment is needed.
6. Xampp-win32-1.7.1 needs to be installed.

CHAPTER 2
REVIEW OF LITERATURE

2.1 Overview

A smart home environment is a technological concept that, according to Cook and Das [1], is "a small world where different kinds of smart device are continuously working to make inhabitants lives more comfortable". Smart environments aim to satisfy the experience of individuals from every environment, by replacing the hazardous work, physical labor, and repetitive tasks with automated agents. The term "smart home" has been defined in several ways. Most broadly, the term can refer to any technology that automates a home-based activity.

The term *smart home* entered the general vocabulary in the 1990s, when Microsoft founder Bill Gates built his computer-controlled "home of the future", with monitoring systems that automatically adjusted in-home lighting, music, pictorial imagery and temperature. The terms smart homes, intelligent homes, home networking have been used for more than a decade to introduce the concept of networking devices and equipment in the house.

Fig 2.1: Smart Home Technology Automation [2]

4

According to the Smart Homes Association the best definition of smart home technology is: "the integration of technology and services through home networking for a better quality of living". Other terms that are related to smart homes are aware house, changeable home, attentive house and ambient intelligence. These terms are used to emphasize that the home environment should be able to respond and modify itself continuously according to its diverse residents and their changeable needs.

The evolution of ubiquitous computing, Internet and consumer electronics have stimulated the rapid growth of services and applications in smart home environment. As Mark Weiser [11] argued that "the most profound technologies are those that disappear" seems suits well the smart home environment characteristics as we could feel the blend of intelligence and technology hiding in the backend, providing comfort to home dwellers with many services and applications.

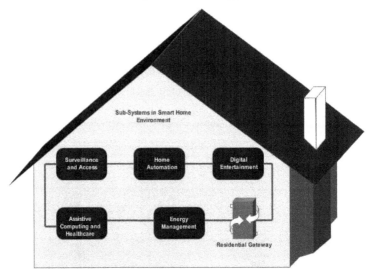

Fig 2.2: Sub-systems in smart home environment [6]

Smart home environment consists of sub-systems which acquire and apply the knowledge about the home dwellers to meet the goal of achieving comfort and efficiency. The subsystems defined in smart home environment are often heterogeneous in nature and developed in isolation. These heterogeneous sub-systems consist of seven main application domains in smart home environment. Figure 2.2 shows the sub-systems defined in smart home environment.

There are five main sub-systems defined in smart home environment. Those sub-systems are:

a) *Surveillance and Access Control* - Keep a watchful eye around your home, even when you are away. With the help of multiple programs user can control and see the status of your home from anywhere via the Internet.

b) *Home Automation Systems* - Light a path for nighttime bathroom trips, have your thermostat start warming the bedroom before you get out of bed and turn on the coffee maker from bed and many more.

c) *Digital Entertainment Systems* - A revolutionary way to enjoy all your media, all around your home. Share your favourite music throughout every zone of your home. No audio rack or expensive proprietary components required.

d) *Assistive Computing and Healthcare* - Could notify the resident when it was time to take medicine, alert the hospital in case of some emergency caused due to unusual conditions.

e) *Energy Management Systems* - Lighting control enhances the enjoyment and value of your home and contributes to savings on your energy bill.

From a user perspective it is important to realize that residents consider their home to be a safe and comfortable place to live in. Sometimes technology is seen as an intruder in their safe environment, residents are afraid to lose control over their home. Some people even fear the use of technology in their home. So technology and the home environment are not naturally a perfect fit. With respect to smart home technology for elderly and disabled people another aspect is important. So the proposed solution is implemented not only to reduce the need to do things but it is also implemented to increase the participation of the resident in an activity.

2.2 Smart Home Software and Technology

Early in 1930s, the perspective of "Machine for Living" was proposed; in 1950s, the term "Automated Home" emerged; nowadays, terms such as "Digital

Home", "Intelligent Home" and "Smart Home" come forth.Smart home technology was developed in 1975, when a company in Scotland developed X10 [2] . Recent advances in computing and communication technologies paved the growth for applications and devices in smart home environment [6]. A Survey of technologies for implementing Smart Home has revealed that it can either be purely wired or purely wireless or it can be both. X10, Z-Wave, ZigBee, and Insteon are some of the technologies for smart home communication. Manufacturers have made alliances with the systems to create the products that use these technologies.

X10 allows compatible products to talk to each other over the already existing electrical wires of a home [9]. All the appliances and devices are receivers, and the means of controlling the system, such as remote controls or keypads, are transmitters. If you want to turn off a lamp in another room, the transmitter will issue a message in numerical code that includes the following: An alert to the system that it's issuing a command, an identifying unit number for the device that should receive the command and a code that contains the actual command, such as "turn off". All of this is designed to happen in less than a second, but X10 does have some limitations. Communicating over electrical lines is not always reliable because the lines get "noisy" from powering other devices. An X10 device could interpret electronic interference as a command and react, or it might not receive the command at all. While X10 devices are still around, other technologies have emerged to compete for our home networking.

Instead of going through the power lines, some systems use radio waves to communicate, which is also how WiFi and cell phone signals operate. However, home automation networks don't need all the juice of a WiFi network because automation commands are short messages. The two most prominent radio networks in home automation are ZigBee and Z-Wave. Both of these technologies are mesh networks, meaning there's more than one way for the message to get to its destination.

Fig 2.3 Smart Home Network Scenario (The dots represent devices that could be connected) [2].

2.2.1 Z-Wave

Z-Wave uses a Source Routing Algorithm to determine the fastest route for messages. Each Z-Wave device is embedded with a code, and when the device is plugged into the system, the network controller recognizes the code, determines its location and adds it to the network. When a command comes through, the controller uses the algorithm to determine how the message should be sent. Because this routing can take up a lot of memory on a network, Z-Wave has developed a hierarchy between devices: Some controllers initiate messages, and some are "slaves," which means they can only carry and respond to messages.

2.2.2 ZigBee

ZigBee name illustrates the mesh networking concept because messages from the transmitter zigzag like bees, looking for the best path to the receiver. While Z-Wave uses a proprietary technology for operating its system, ZigBee platform is based on the standard set by the Institute for Electrical and Electronics Engineers (IEEE) for wireless personal networks [2]. This means any company can build a

8

ZigBee-compatible product without paying licensing fees for the technology behind it, which may eventually give ZigBee an advantage in the marketplace. Like Z-Wave, ZigBee has fully functional devices (or those that route the message) and reduced function devices (or those that don't).

2.2.3 Insteon

Using a wireless network provides more flexibility for placing devices, but like electrical lines, they might have interference. Insteon offers a way for your home network to communicate over both electrical wires and radio waves, making it a dual mesh network. If the message isn't getting through on one platform, it will try the other. Instead of routing the message, an Insteon device will broadcast the message, and all devices pick up the message and broadcast it until the command is performed. The devices act like peers, as opposed to one serving as an instigator and another as a receptor. This means that the more Insteon devices that are installed on a network, the stronger the message will be. The idea behind implementation of this project is based on Insteon technology.

Remote control gives you the convenience of controlling lighting, appliances, security systems and consumer electronics from wherever you happen to be at the time, like your couch, car, bed or even outside your home. There are several different "methods" of controlling devices remotely.

Table 2.1: Comparison of Smart home Technologies

Remote Technology	Products	Advantages	Disadvantages	Popular Applications
Power line	X10	Inexpensive and can cover entire house through already fitted powerline.	Noise is induced and thus may require noise filters & phase	Mostly used to control Lighting, appliances and also for security reason.

			couplers	
Radio-Frequency (RF)	Z-Wave , ZigBee	Works through walls that means doesn't have difficulty to signal devices across the walls.	Cannot cover Long distant devices, more expensive than X10	Mostly used for controlling Garage doors, and also for computer networking
Power Line & RF	Insteon	It works with inheritance to X10 products, Inexpensive, can cover entire house, no noise filters required, works through walls, maximum speed and reliability, adding new products increases more reliability.	No Disadvantages found. Compared to X10, Z-Wave and ZigBee it is better.	Mostly used to control Lighting, Home appliances but also can used for controlling computer and computer connected devices.

2.3 Setting up a Smart Home

X10, Insteon, ZigBee and Z-Wave just provide the technology for smart home communication. Manufacturers have made alliances with these systems to create the products that use the technology [2]. Here are some examples of smart home products and their functions.

1. **Cameras** will track your home's exterior even if it's pitch-black outside.

2. Plug your tabletop lamp into a **dimmer** instead of the wall socket, and you can brighten and dim at the push of a button.
3. A **Video door phone** provides more than a doorbell -- you get a picture of who's at the door.
4. **Motion sensors** will send an alert when there's motion around your house, and they can even tell the difference between pets and burglars.
5. **Door handles** can open with scanned fingerprints or a four-digit code, eliminating the need to fumble for house keys.
6. **Audio systems** distribute the music from your stereo to any room with connected speakers.
7. **Channel modulators** take any video signal -- from a security camera to your favorite television station -- and make it viewable on every television in the house.
8. **Remote controls**, **keypads** and **tabletop controllers** are the means of activating the smart home applications. Devices also come with **built-in web servers** that allow you to access their information online.

When designing a smart home, you can do as much or as little home automation as you want. You could begin with a lighting starter kit and add on security devices later. If you want to start with a bigger system, it's a good idea to design carefully how the home will work, particularly if rewiring or renovation will be required. In addition, you'll want to place strategically the nodes of the wireless networks so that they have a good routing range. The cost of a smart home varies depending on how smart the home is. If you build the smart home gradually, starting with a basic lighting system, it might cost you five thousand to ten thousand rupees depending upon the functionality of the system.

2.4 Smart Home Advantages

Smart homes obviously have the ability to make life easier and more convenient. Home networking can also provide peace of mind. Whether you're at work or on vacation, the smart home will alert you to what's going on, and security systems can be built to provide an immense amount of help in an emergency. For example, not only would a resident be woken with notification of a fire alarm, the smart home would also unlock doors, dial the fire department and light the path to safety.

Smart homes also provide some energy efficiency savings. Because systems like Z-Wave and ZigBee put some devices at a reduced level of functionality, they can go to "sleep" and wake up when commands are given. Electric bills go down when lights are automatically turned off when a person leaves the room, and rooms can be heated or cooled based on who's there at any given moment. One smart homeowner boasted her heating bill was about one third less than a same-sized normal home. Some devices can track how much energy each appliance is using and command it to use less.

Smart home technology promises tremendous benefits for an elderly person living alone. Smart homes could notify the resident when it was time to take medicine, alert the hospital if the resident fell and track how much the resident was eating. If the elderly person was a little forgetful, the smart home would perform tasks such as shutting off the water before a tub overflowed or turning off the oven if the cook had wandered away. It also allows adult children who might live elsewhere to participate in the care of their aging parent. Easy-to control automated systems would provide similar benefits to those with disabilities or a limited range of movement.

CHAPTER 3
DESCRIPTION

3.1 Smart Home System

Nowadays, the communications becomes very simple, fast, interactive and more compact, that makes the global as a small village. So it is very easy for anyone to subscribe in the local or global telecommunication networks with Internet or through individual mobile phone device. With today's and tomorrow's wireless technologies, such as IEEE 802.11, Blue tooth and GPRS, mobile devices will frequently be in close and interactive communication. Smart home technology makes remote communication with the surrounding possible via the Internet, ordinary fixed telephones or mobile phones [4]. As the Internet and home networking technologies are developing rapidly, more users want to control their home appliances from a remote location, i.e. from outside the home. This system proposes two subsystems: One controlling device over internet using IP protocol and second controlling device over internet using GPRS protocol.

The system for controlling home appliance remotely have used web server as the interface between user and home network. Although the system that adopts web server offers many advantages, this approach requires a fix IP (Internet Protocol) address and remote user require high-speed connection in order to access the web interface due to the heavy loaded Graphical User Interface (GUI) and interactive components of the web interface. Home Automation system uses GPRS mobile phone wherein the home device is connected to the serial port of the computer through the interfacing switching circuit. GUI (graphical user interface) is hosted on web server and can be accessed on GPRS mobile phone, through which user can control as well as monitor his home appliance. PC remote control with small mobile device is a challenging topic of mobile/ubiquitous computing. Enabling user to use data and functions stored in/served by their home PCs from anywhere with small mobile devices is beneficial because users can access the data/functions at any time they want without carrying heavy notebook PCs.

This system consists of components (shown in figure 2):-

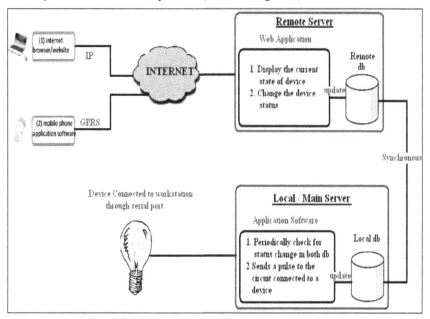

Fig 3.1:- Model of Smart Home System

1. **Browser/Website** – This is a user interface for accessing the web application. This interface can be used to check and update the status of registered devices at the same time or at a specified time in the future. This would update the remote server database by sending the required commands to the remote web application.

2. **Mobile device** – The mobile application software consists of a user interface for accessing the web application. This interface can be used to check and update the status of devices that the user has registered. The application connects to the web application using GPRS connection and updates the remote server database by sending the required commands to the remote web application.

3. **Local or Main Server**-This unit contains the software components through

14

which the device is controlled and home security is monitored. The software component periodically checks for status changes for device in remote and local server database. On receiving changes in database, the software on local machine sends a pulse (character) to the circuit connected to the home device, which in turn updates the device status accordingly. This unit is very much important because it helps user to access the device locally and also can change its status without internet connection. So this component helps user to overcome one of the constraints of the system.

4. **Web server database (remote database)** – This database is stored on the remote server. This database contains records for the device's current status. It is kept in synchronous with the local server on the user machine and is checked periodically by the local software component in order to control the local device.

5. **Local database** – This is a database that stores the status of the device locally. This database is kept in synchronous with remote database.

GPRS is a protocol, which has emerged to allow cellular phones on the GSM network to access the Internet [2]. This is opening up a whole world of opportunities for cellular phones as they can now communicate data to anywhere for relatively small cost. Using GPRS as the main communication protocol for the house server rather than SMS would improve the system as it would become more accessible to other devices and protocols via the internet and also it would allow more affordable data transfer within the cellular system.

Another use of GPRS for this application could be implementing a web server on the microcontroller so the house could be accessed by any other devices over the internet, although security would have to be made extra strict. The system is capable enough to enable user via web interface to change the condition of the home appliance according to the user's needs and requirements. The state of connected device is also represented. A single click changes the state of the device (off to on and vice versa), and the change in state is updated as it occurs.

3.2 Working of Smart Home System

The system has two modules wherein the home device is connected to the serial port of the computer through the interfacing switching circuit. First module requires a fix IP (Internet Protocol) address and remote user require high-speed connection in order to access the web interface and other interactive components of the web. Second module, where GUI (graphical user interface) is hosted on web server and can be accessed on a GPRS enabled mobile phone through a mobile application.

The website browser/mobile application access the web application located at the remote server via internet/GPRS. Once logged in, all devices and their current status are displayed. Using the web application user interface, the user can update the device status at the same time or at a specified time in the future and once the update has been made, the application will then update its remote server database. The software on the main server periodically checks its own database with the remote server database and synchronizes changes accordingly, i.e. it periodically checks for status change by querying the remote server and matches them with the main server. On receiving change in local database, the software on main server sends a pulse (character) to the circuit connected to the home device, which in turn updates the device status. The software then updates the local database so that both local and remote database is synchronized. Even if the device is turned on /turned off manually by user at home, this would be reflected in the local database of workstation and thus the remote database is updated accordingly. So that whenever user logged in to check the status he would get the updated state of the device.

CHAPTER 4
IMPLEMENTATION

4.1 Smart Home System Design

Smart homes looks great on paper and very exciting to work with but many people are still afraid to use it. A smart home probably sounds like a nightmare to those people not comfortable with computers. It may be your fear that if you try to turn on the television in your smart home, lights will start flashing, and this does happen occasionally. (Power outages, however, activate backup battery and safe mode, which means you, can still perform tasks like unlocking a door manually). One of the challenges of installing a smart home system is balancing the complexity of the system against the usability of the system. While implementing the system, we have taken care of few factors:

1. How large will the system be?

We wanted to build a low cost home automation system used to remotely control home light. So it's a small system with one device controlled through web and mobile application.

2. What kinds of components are parts of the system?

They are basic, such as a light, fan, washing machine or air conditioner.

3. How intuitive will the system be to a non-user?

Password protection is used to block the unauthorized from accessing to the server.

4. How many people will be required to use the system?

As such one member is sufficient to use the system. But as the system is designed for home all the family members can have access to the system.

5. Who will know how to operate the system?

The system is designed keeping in mind the nature of a lay man user so the user interface is very easy to understand and operate. Any user comfortable with computers can easily operate the system.

4.2 Functional Design

Level 0 DFD for Smart Home System Application:

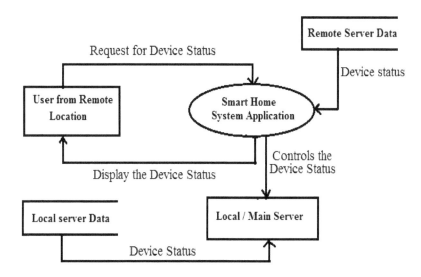

Fig 4.1 Level 0 DFD for Smart Home System Application

Level 0 DFD shows that user request for device status and if required change the status of the device. It shows that the smart home system application process requires remote server data. The arrows representing data flow are labeled to show what data is being used. Device status is received from the remote server data store & from local/main server data store and is kept synchronous in order to control the device request of the user.

Level 1 DFD for Smart Home System Processing:

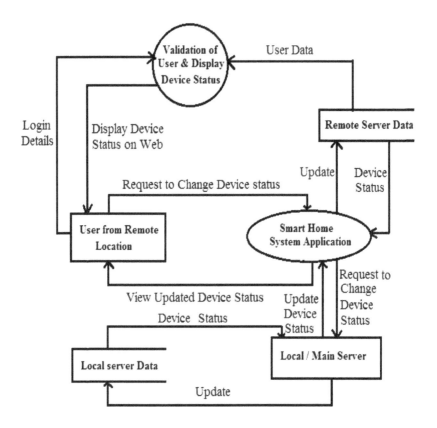

Fig 4.2 Level 1 DFD for Smart Home System Processing

Level 1 DFD for Validation of User & display of Device Status:

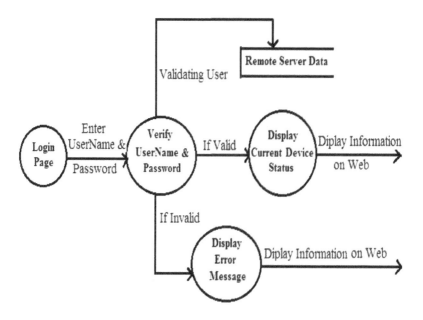

Fig 4.3 Level 1 DFD for Validation of User & display of Device Status

Level 2 DFD for Status Change & Status Update:

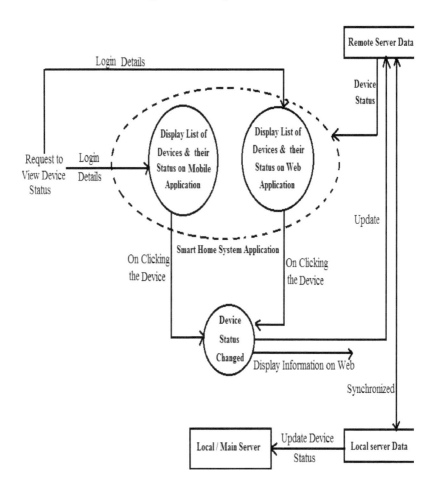

Fig 4.4 Level 2 DFD for Status Change & Update Processing

4.3 Design Considerations

4.3.1 Hardware Design & Implementation

The Signal (i.e. the Character) coming from the PC is connected to the Drive board via (DB-9 Pin) Serial port. The IC MAX232 is used to convert the RS232 signal into TTL voltage level, which are used for receive and transmit signal of microcontrollers. The signal received from MAX232 is further provided to Microcontroller 89V51RD2BN (40 Pin IC). RS232 signal is not compatible with microcontroller hence we use MAX232.

Fig 4.5: Hardware circuit Board

The following Pseudo code is to receive Signal (i.e. the Character A or B) coming from the PC on output port (PORT-2) of Microcontroller:

Function ReceiveByteSerially is

Input: integer RI, char SBUF

1. If RI is 0, wait until data is received

2. Clear the Flag

3. Return Serial Data

4. If SBUF= 'A' , Microcontroller is set high

5. High output drive the appliance connected to be ON.

End ReceiveByteSerially

The microcontroller receives Character 'A' from RS232 through IC MAX232; with this output port (PORT-2) of Microcontroller is set high. The High output is further provided to the relay to drive the appliances which are connected with the interface. Further PORT-1 is connected to the LCD display, when the appliance is ON, LCD display show the corresponding device status. It also sends back the ON status of the device to the PC.

When the Microcontroller receives Character 'B' the PORT-2 of microcontroller is set low and the corresponding relay of the appliance is deactivated. With this the LCD display shows the current status of the corresponding appliances. And also sends the OFF status back to the PC. All the IC's and components are driven on a supply voltage of 5V. Relay is provided with 12V supply.

The following Pseudo code is to Send Signal (i.e. the Character A or B) coming from output port (PORT-2) of Microcontroller as an acknowledgement to the PC:

Function SendByteSerially is

Input: integer TI, char SBUF

      1. Load data to serial buffer Register

      2. If TI is 0, wait for transmission to complete

      3. Clear transmission Interrupt flag

End SendByteSerially

4.3.2 Software Design & Implementation

4.3.2.1 Smart Home System Software

The implementation of the system is carried out using Java runtime Environment and PHP.

1. Java Runtime Environment

The Java Runtime Environment (JRE), also known as Java Runtime, is part of the Java Development Kit (JDK), a set of programming tools for developing Java applications. The Java Runtime Environment provides the minimum requirements for executing a Java application; it consists of the Java Virtual Machine (JVM), core classes, and supporting files.J2EE is yet another acronym in the world of computing. This one stands for *Java 2 Platform, Enterprise Edition*. Its significance will become clear once we trace its lineage. First of all, Java is a programming language developed by Sun Microsystems, one of the giants of the industry. The Java Platform is a virtual machine, a processor look-alike that translates computerized instructions into functions.

The Java language is such that it allows cross-platform communication between multiple kinds of devices. For example, a programmer can develop Java code on a desktop computer and expect it to run on other computers, routers, and even mobile phones, as long as those devices are Java-enabled. This portability is described by the Sun acronym WORA, which stands for "Write once, run anywhere." A large number of mainframes, computers, mobile phones, and other electronic devices operate using the Java Platform. The *2* in the acronym J2EE stands for *Version 2*. As with many software applications, J2EE is Java Platform Version 2. Actually, the number 2 is often dropped nowadays, so J2EE becomes Java EE. Traditionally, though, it's still J2EE. Now, *EE* in J2EE stands for *Enterprise Edition*, which is a powerful form of the Java Platform. Sun has created three editions so far. The most precise is the Micro Edition, which is used for mobile phones and PDAs. Following form, this can be abbreviated as Java ME.

The middle edition is the Standard Edition, which can run on mobile devices, laptops and desktop computers. The abbreviated name of this edition is Java SE. Building our way up the pyramid, we come at last to the Enterprise Edition, which includes all the functionality of the Micro Edition and the

Standard Edition and also features routines and subroutines designed specifically for servers and mainframes. One prime benefit of the J2EE, despite the assumption of such a powerful set of source code, is that it is available for free. You can download it right now from the Sun Microsystems website. Third-party open-source tools are available to help you as well, including Apache Tomcat. Unless you are running your own multiple-workstation server system or mainframe, however, you are unlikely to encounter or have a need for J2EE.

2.PHP

PHP is just one of many popular Web server side open source scripting languages. It is widely used for Web application development. There are over half million server pages developed by PHP. It is still growing very fast. PHP is often embedded into HTML to enhance functions of HTML. PHP allows you to interact with a HTML page dynamically. PHP collect data from page where user provides and then process and utilize data to create a dynamic home page output.

PHP can do all tasks that ASP and JSP can do plus it is free. PHP is so popular because of the following reasons:

- PHP is Open Source and free
- PHP is much compact than Java and .NET in term of its system size
- PHP is portable and runs on Linux, Windows, and Mac platforms
- PHP is a server-side script language easy to be adopted
- PHP has fast connections to popular databases compared with Perl
- PHP is integrated with the Open Source MySql database
- PHP is an OO interpreter language
- PHP Web pages work with all popular major browsers
- PHP has integrated linking to XML PDF, SWF, and Java for dynamic creation and processing
- PHP syntax is similar to C, Perl and java.

PHP marries HTML well because PHP is designed to be used along with HTML. You can embed PHP into HTML document, or put HTML tags in PHP coding seamlessly. In addition, PHP gets alone with MySql very well. These two make up the best combination for data-driven Web application cross-platform. PHP can also support a massive number of databases, including Informix, Oracle, Sybase, and ODBC drivers.

4.3.2.2 Smart Home System Functional Units

The idea of remote home control was implemented by dividing the entire system into the following three functional units.

1. Java based unit

This unit uses the RXTX package for serial port communication so as to send bits to the serial port to which the electronic kit is connected and which is intern connected to the device. The RXTX package provides with function's like connect (), serialEvent (), and write () which is used to connect to, read from and write to the serial port.

The other important thing that this unit does is it keeps both the remote server and the main server synchronized. This is achieved with help of a thread running at the main server which constantly sends a request at specified time intervals to the remote server and keeps updating the local database depending on the response that it gets from the remote server and also updates the remote database whenever a change is made to the local database by using the same request/response mechanism. Here the thread is used to synchronize both the server database with respect to two things: most recent device status and last updated time of that device if any. This unit also allows additional appliances to be added to the system.

The graphical user interface designed to read the current state of the device from Main server to which the device is actually connected:

a) Graphical User Interface for reading device status from main server:

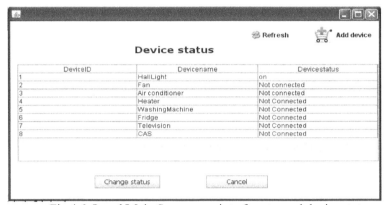

Fig 4.6: Local/Main Server user interface to read device status.

A device status can be read using the above interface and if needed user can change the status at the same time or at a specified time in the future by clicking the "Change status" button. This interface not only helps the user to access the device locally but also can activate/deactivate the device in absence of an internet connection.

The following is the Flowchart to show working of Java thread which is running on the Main /Local Server:

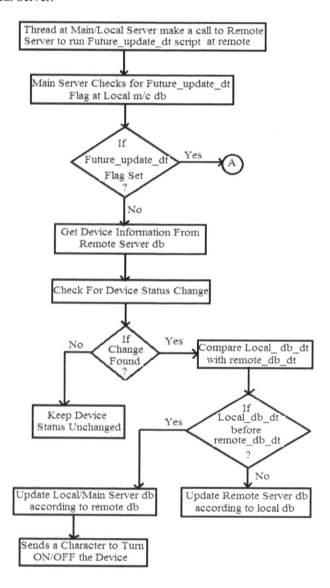

Fig 4.7: Flowchart for Change Device Status at a particular Instance

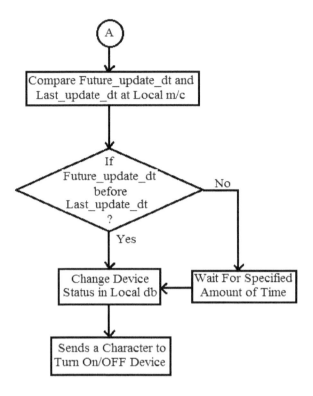

Fig 4.8: Flowchart for Change Device Status at a specified time in the future

2. Web unit

This unit uses PHP and MySql to maintain synchronization between the local database and the remote database. Using the in-built query system of the PHP framework appropriate responses are provided to the requests made by the Java module and the Mobile module. An authentication system is used to ensure that the requests made are valid and secure. An HTML/CSS GUI serves as a front-end for the user, where the user can remotely access their devices through browser, can check the device status and if needed can change the status.

b) Graphical User Interface for Reading Device Status from Remote Server:

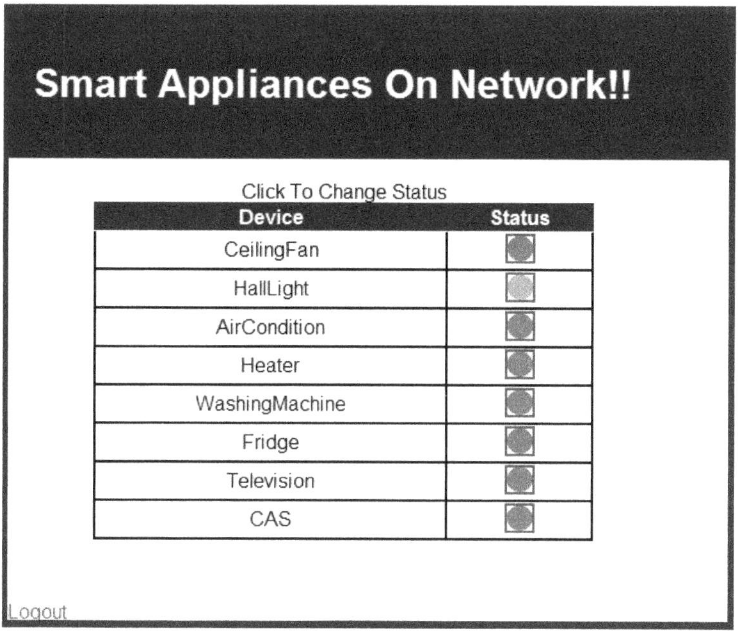

Smart Appliances On Network!!

Click To Change Status

Device	Status
CeilingFan	◉
HallLight	◉
AirCondition	◉
Heater	◉
WashingMachine	◉
Fridge	◉
Television	◉
CAS	◉

Logout

Fig 4.9: Remote Server User Interface to Read Device Status using Web Application.

A device status can be read using the above interface through web application and if needed user can change the status at the same time or at a specified time in the future by clicking the "Green/Red" image icon in front of respective device.

c) **Graphical User Interface for Changing device status from remote server:**

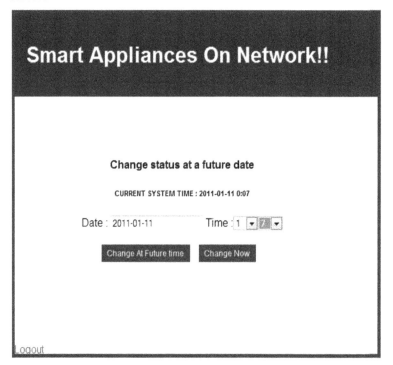

Fig 4.10: Remote Server User Interface to Change Device Status using Web Application.

User can change the device status at the same time or at a specified time in the future using the above user Interface. Current System date and time is provided on the page for the user even Validation checks are provided so that user cannot enter a past date and time.

3. Mobile unit

This unit uses J2me (Java 2 micro edition) which is used to develop applications for cell phones which supports java. J2me is used to create a midlet which makes HTTP connections. J2me supports RMS for storing session data in cell phone but due to security reasons none of the data is stored in the device. User has to go through the login screen during every session. On correct authentication respective web services is called and the data received in response is parsed by OnResponse_parser ().

If the user is authenticated, server sends data related to the appliances registered and their current status (ON/OFF). This data is parsed and displayed in the form of a list. List contains: Name of the registered appliance and its current state (ON/OFF). If the user change the status of any registered device, again OnResponse_parser () plays role in parsing the response data. If the server responds success the change in device state is updated and is shown on mobile screen. If the device is not registered it simply gives a message notifying that the device is not connected.

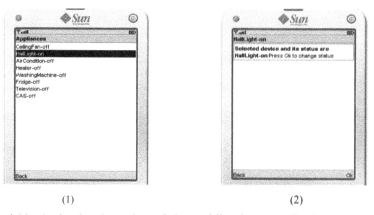

(1)   (2)

Fig 4.11: A simulated version of the mobile phone application - (1) List of appliances with their current status, (2) Device selected to change status.

CHAPTER 5
RESULTS AND DISCUSSION

The proposed system characteristic involves remote controlling of appliances and has many advantages such as availability and ease of users. The user can access the home appliance from anywhere through Internet technology thus making the system location independent. The system contains low cost components easily available which cuts down the overall system cost. The ease of deployment is due to wireless mode of communication. The system integration is simple and is also scalable and extensible.The key drivers for this application will be ease of use and the penetration of network enabled home devices/appliances. The primary business opportunity will be to bundle home automation services with other residential services.

Table 5.1: Results of Appliance Control Subsystem

Appliance	Received Character	System Response
Hall light	SBUF= A	Light is Turned ON
	SBUF=B	Light is Turned OFF

Achieved analytical results:-

1. System allowed the provision of accessing the appliance remotely; at present system has access to one device i.e. Hall Light.
2. Remote Controlling capability of the system allowed user to switch on/off through simulating the appliance as directed by the incoming Character.

Constraints of System:

The system functionality is based on Internet technology so the technological constraints must be kept in mind. The system is vulnerable to power failure but this disruption can be avoided by attaching the voltage source thus allowing users to avail the great advantage of this system.

CHAPTER 6
CONCLUSION AND FUTURE WORK

Smart homes have the ability to make life easier and more convenient by achieving ones peace of mind. This system introduces a low cost, secure, ubiquitously accessible, auto-configurable, remotely controlled solution for automation of home. The system is designed to simplify inhabitants life by bringing different technologies at home together into one complete elegant easily use solution. This is a practical, reliable remote home control system that fits into any home, new or old, large or small, and within budget. It is entirely scalable, so you can start with the basic system and upgrade over time and solutions that favor change in needs and your imaginations. The approach discussed in this report is novel and has achieved the target to control home appliance remotely.

Application of the System:

Increasing number of smart, intelligent and communication capable devices that allow users to control and monitor events (remotely) are fast emerging. There is an increasing need and demand for the remote management of home utilities and services. The emergence of home networking along with the broadband access would enable a host of service to be delivered to the home. No matter the extent of your travels for business or pleasure this system will always have power to monitor and control home remotely. Our System can also be customized to respond to the following needs such as

1. Pet lovers are also making use of remote access. They are able to set up home surveillance by adding a webcam to the home computer which they can access remotely form work or from a mobile device in order to check on their pets and ensure they are alright. This is useful if you have to leave an animal for a longer period of time than it is accustomed to.

2. The same type of technology has also been used by people wanting to check on a new babysitter, functioning much the same way as a Nanny Cam, except you

can have a real time view rather than watching recorded footage at a later date. Parents are also making use of remote control software to access their children's computers, keeping track of their internet activity without the need to constantly hover around them. This offers children a greater sense of freedom while still affording parents a sense of security and peace of mind.

PC remote access offers such a wide range of possibilities that many people who install the remote control software for one purpose, such as being able to work from home, often end up utilizing it in day to day life for a variety of purposes. Once a remote access connection has been established the possibilities are endless and are limited only by the user's own imagination.

Future Work:

The basic level of home appliance control and remote monitoring has been implemented. The system is extensible and more levels can be further developed by providing remote access through GSM network [4]. This method is another alternative to extend the remote access range of a smart home network. The host server will be equipped with a GSM modem to enable communication to client mobile devices through the GSM network cloud, bypassing the Internet connection entirely.

While the Internet connection on a mobile device is dependent on network coverage, i.e. a Wi-Fi hotspot or UMTS subscription, it also means that the mobile device used must be a high end model with access to the Internet and with browser capabilities; i.e. a pocket pc or a smart phone. Although most of the current generation of released mobile phone models nowadays have this capability, it will be an added advantage if the application can also work without being dependable on an Internet connection. Sending and receiving commands to smart home devices through the GSM network will require the use of Short Messaging Service, SMS and hence will be a more expensive solution as compared to the use of Internet.

However, with this solution, lower end mobile phone models, in fact any mobile phone that can send out SMS will be able to utilize the smart home remote access application. It can also be a good alternative for the user to use in cases where Internet coverage is not available for the mobile phone.

GLOSSARY

Automation

The techniques and equipment used to achieve automatic operation or control.

Ambient Intelligence

It refers to electronic environments that are sensitive and responsive to the presence of people wherein devices work in concert to support people in carrying out their everyday life activities easily.

Bluetooth

It is a proprietary open wireless technology standard for exchanging data over short distances (using short wavelength radio transmissions) from fixed and mobile devices, creating personal area networks (PANs) with high levels of security.

Cellular System

It is a radio network made up of a number of radio cells (or just cells) each served by a fixed transmitter, normally known as a base station. These cells are used to cover different areas in order to provide radio coverage over a wider area than the area of one cell.

Digital Home

A fully automated home is known as digital Home. It uses computing devices and home appliances that conform to some common standard for internetworking so that everything can be controlled by computer.

GPRS- General Packet Radio Service

It is a packet-based wireless communication service that promises data rates from 56 up to 114 Kbps and continuous connection to the Internet for mobile phone and computer users.

GSM- Global System for Mobile Communications

GSM is the world's most popular standard for mobile telephony systems. Cell phones use a cell phone service carrier's GSM network by searching for cell phone towers in the nearby area.

HTTP-Hyper Text Transfer Protocol

It provides a standard for Web browsers and servers to communicate. The definition of HTTP is a technical specification of a network protocol that software must implement.

Home Automation

Home automation is the use of one or more computers to control basic home functions and features automatically and sometimes remotely. An automated home is sometimes called a smart home.

IP- Internet Protocol

It is the method or protocol by which data is sent from one computer to another on the Internet. Each computer (known as a host) on the Internet has at least one IP address that uniquely identifies it from all other computers on the Internet.

Insteon

Insteon technology is a dual-band mesh topology employing AC-power lines and a radio-frequency (RF) protocol to communicate with and automate home electronic devices and appliances, which normally work independently.

Instigator

A person who initiates a course of action says for example a transmitter.

J2EE- Java 2 Platform, Enterprise Edition

It is a Java platform designed for the mainframe-scale computing typical of large enterprises. J2EE simplifies application development and decreases the need for programming and programmer training by creating standardized, reusable modular components and by enabling the tier to handle many aspects of programming automatically.

J2me- Java 2 micro edition

It is a technology that allows programmers to use the Java programming language and related tools to develop programs for mobile wireless information devices such as cellular phones.

Mesh Network

Mesh networking is a type of networking wherein each node in the network may act as an independent router, regardless of whether it is connected to another network or not.

Midlet

A Midlet is an application that uses the Mobile Information Device Profile (MIDP) of the Connected Limited Device Configuration (CLDC) for the Java ME environment. It is a Java program for embedded devices, more specifically the J2ME virtual machine.

RMS

The J2ME record management system (RMS) provides a mechanism through which Midlet can persistently store data and retrieve it later. In a record-oriented approach, J2ME RMS comprises multiple record stores.

Source Routing

It is a technique whereby the sender of a packet can specify the route that a packet should take through the network.

Ubiquitous Computing

Ubicomp is a post-desktop model of human-computer interaction in which information processing has been thoroughly integrated into everyday objects and activities.

WiFi

A local area network that uses high frequency radio signals to transmit and receive data over distances of a few hundred feet uses Ethernet protocol.

Wireless Personal Network

It is a personal area network - a network for interconnecting devices centered on an individual person's workspace - in which the connections are wireless. Typically, a wireless personal area network uses some technology that permits communication within about 10 meters - in other words, a very short range.

X10

It is a communication protocol for remote control of electrical devices. It uses power line wiring for signaling and control, where the signals involve short RF bursts representing digital information.

ZigBee

A standard for short-distance, low-data-rate communications using the frequencies and physical and data layers of the IEEE 802.15.4 PHY specification. Created and maintained by the ZIGBEE Alliance Group.

Z-Wave

It is a proprietary wireless communications protocol designed for home automation, specifically to remote control applications in residential and light commercial environments.

REFERENCES

[1] Cook, Diane; Das, Sajal, "Smart Environments: Technology, Protocols and Applications", 2005.

[2]Rosslin John Robles and Tai-hoon Kim, "Applications, Systems and methods in Smart Home Technology: A review", International Journal of Advanced Science and Technology Vol. 15, February, 2010.

[3]M J Van Der Werff, W L Xu, X, X GUI, "Activation of Home Automation System via Mobile Technology", New Zealand.

[4]Safiyya Rusli, Mehrdad Dianati, "Mobile Access to Smart Home Network" University of Surrey Guildford, United Kingdom.

[5] Molly Edmonds "How Smart Homes Work - Setting Up a Smart Home" http://home.howstuffworks.com/home-improvement/energy-efficiency/smart-home1.htm

[6]Thinagaran Perumal, Abdul Ramli, Chui Yew Leong, Shattri Mansor, Khairulmizam Samsudin, "Interoperability for Smart Home Environment Using Web Services", International Journal of Smart Home,Vol. 2, No. 4, October, 2008.

[7]Malik Sikandar Khiyal, Aihab Khan, and Erum Shehzadi, "SMS Based Wireless Home Appliance Control System (HACS) for Automating Appliances and Security", Issues in Informing Science and Information Technology, Volume 6, 2009.

[8]Satish Gupta, "A White Paper on Home Networking", Wipro technologies, Bangalore.

[9]X10 Technology, http://www.x10.com

[10] Anne-mie A. G. Sponselee, Ben A. M. Schouten, and Don G. Bouwhuis, "Effective Use of Smart Home Technology to Increase Well-being", 2008.

[11] M.Weiser, "The Computer of 21st Century", Scientific American, 1991.

www.ingramcontent.com/pod-product-compliance
Lightning Source LLC
LaVergne TN
LVHW042352060326
832902LV00006B/550